The Past That Follows

By Liza A Perez

authorHOUSE®

AuthorHouse™
1663 Liberty Drive
Bloomington, IN 47403
www.authorhouse.com
Phone: 1-800-839-8640

First published by AuthorHouse 9/2/2010

ISBN: 978-1-4490-8746-3 (sc)
ISBN: 978-1-4490-8747-0 (e)

Library of Congress Control Number: 2010912614

Printed in the United States of America

This book is printed on acid-free paper.

The Past That Follows

By Liza A Perez

ONCE UPON A TIME in a small country town lived a family of twelve. They were eight girls and four boys. Everything seemed pretty normal. Mom and Dad worked. Dad worked at a door factory and mom took care of all of us kids.

Most everyone went to school. I used to watch mom do the cooking, cleaning, ironing, and so forth. Everything had to get done by the time my dad got home. Dad always had a belief women were to stay home and take care of the house. While men went to work and brought home the bread. After everyone came home from school, chores had to be done. Dad would get upset if chores at home were not done. He always said, "There was no excuse for a home to be a mess with eight women in the house." Laundry seemed to never end, we had to use a scrub board to wash our clothes and hang our clothes out to dry. We chopped wood for winter and the men would go hunting, fishing, or anything just to make ends meet.

However, I began to realize at a real young age that things were starting to look weird. I mean as a kid you expect to play with toys, like dolls or at least a swing set. Well this little girl was growing up without a lot of things. We even had to learn to mow a yard while the guys worked. I don't remember any of us really having a normal childhood.

I was five years old when I started school. My first day was hard, I cried because I didn't want my mom home alone. And when you are living in the country, which is the middle of nowhere. Well for me it was scary. So I got over the fear real quick, by beginning to make friends. I always would sit down and play. However, I noticed how the schools had all these books and toys. I would listen and hear how some of my friends would laugh and talk about my clothes, how I would smell, and made fun of my shoes. I admit I wasn't rich by any means. But it sure did hurt that I couldn't fit in. I felt I was a poor little girl trying to fit in a rich mans world. I even notice that the teachers would treat other students differently. If some students were the rich looking type well they had more of an advantage. They could do special things for the teachers. I felt like an outcast, it was just another thing I would have to get use to. I thought it was bad at school.

Once the school day ended, I was excited to go home. The moment we got home. Well it was time for homework then chores. Well after everything was done, even the cooking

Well I noticed Dad was always late from work. He was never on time for a meal, so we always ate without dad. After we were done eating, dishes we washed and put them away. Dad would come home at late hours of the night. He always came home drunk, but we were always in bed. Dad would start arguing with mom. He would start hitting on my mom because his food was cold. I would cover my ears, because I hated hearing my dad yell at my mom and making her cry. This became an everyday thing, but when the night was over it was a relief. Because that meant it was time for us to go to school and dad to go to work.

We began to dread night fall, because we knew every night it was dad coming home drunk and mom crying. Everything became a routine. As I began to get older, something else started happening and I didn't know why?

But I remember sleeping in my bed one night. I felt something awful. I felt like my voice box was taken away and my body was so numb that I couldn't move. I felt someone's hands touching my body. Tears rolled down my eyes, however not a yell or a scream left my mouth. Once it was all over all I seen was a shadow leave my room, couldn't really see who it was at the time. But I was so relieved when it was over. At least I thought it was. I also remember I would wake up soaking wet at times. I would pee in bed just about everyday. I was so scared to walk to the bathroom which was outside in the next field. We lived out in the country so we did not have inside restrooms like we do today.

As each day came and went it seemed as normal as it could be. We would have to milk the goats, gather the eggs out of the barn, and feed the pigs. Mom would save money anyway she could. However, Mom was so busy with keeping the house clean and cooking. I don't believe mom really knew everything that was going on. It was a routine day-in and day-out. Dads off to work, kids off to school. While, mom stayed home doing laundry and cleaning the house.

We would come home after school do homework, help mom with getting supper ready. We would eat without Dad like always and go to bed by nine and hear the yelling and arguments every time dad got home.

Once the lights were off, everyone was asleep. The dark shadow would arrive once again. Hands would slowly go up my legs, as tears rolled down my cheeks. I felt as if my voice box was pulled out of me, every time this happened.

One time I was able to move just a small bit. The shadow would once again leave my room. This would happen until the age of ten, or at least until moving day.

I noticed that everyone at home was excited. I didn't really know what the reason was. Until, I saw everyone was carrying boxes to a truck and our beds were being taken apart. I began to cry because I didn't want to leave the old house.

However, I kept hearing how big our new house was and we were going to have a huge yard and all. It seemed like it was going to be ok, at least until we seen it.

So we finally got to the new house. Then we started to hear stories about the house being an old funeral home. It had an upstairs with four rooms up there. I wondered where everyone was to sleep. There were twelve of us and only six rooms. We already knew the boys were getting their own rooms. Mom and Dad were getting theirs. So that left two bedrooms where all of us girls had to sleep which meant. I didn't have to sleep being scared.

Well we noticed it was starting to get real cloudy. So we had to rush to get everything put away. After everything was done, the rain started to pour outside. We thought being in the new home was going to be so much better. Boy! Were we ever wrong! We were all lying in our beds and all of a sudden we felt drops of water falling from the ceiling onto our beds.

We had to get a huge sheet of plastic to cover our beds so we could cover up with our blankets to get some sleep. But, when we woke up, the rooms had pans filled with water. There was not a room in the house that didn't have a leak in it at all. The house always smelled like mildew, the windows were broken, and our rooms had no doors.

People would pass by our house and throw rocks just to bust another window. When we go to school our classmates would laugh at us and ask us questions like, "Aren't y'all the ones that moved into the funeral home or haunted house?" They would also ask, "Is it scary?" and I would say "No!"

Everyday it was the same jokes. If it wasn't about our house, it was about the car my mom drove, the truck my dad had, the way we smelled, or even about my teeth. But, our classmates always had something to poke fun about.

Well school was over, and some kids would follow us home from school just to see if they could come in the house. Just to see what it looked like. Some thought they wouldn't come out alive, others thought it was cool. Even after that the jokes still kept going on.

Well we were home and as usual chores needed to get done. Homework needed to get finished, but 9 o'clock was the deadline. Dad wouldn't have us staying up past 9:00 doing homework. Dad didn't care if we had other chores to do either. Well homework was done at least as much as we could do even if we were not done with it all, it was time for bed. We all said good night before we go to our rooms. Kiss mom and if dad was home we would give him a kiss as well.

Then right when everyone is asleep. I felt this awful feeling once again. Crawling up my legs and the pain was horriable. I couldn't breathe. I couldn't even move. Seems the more I tried to scream, the more it seemed my voice wasn't around. Nothing would even come out of my mouth. I didn't know what was going on. I was scared to even say anything. I didn't know if this was a good or bad thing. I didn't know what to do.

I had never felt so uncomfortable. I could only wonder if it was a normal feeling or if I was the only one going through this. I mean I did have seven more sisters and I'm sure I wasn't the only one that ever felt the shadow in the night.

However, sunlight was starting to break and another day of school was already here. It felt more relaxed being at school it seemed as if I felt safe there. But I started to notice every time I tried to do classwork the more distracted I would get. Because my mind would wonder off to the night before. The feeling of trying to find out what this shadow was and why it was always coming to my bedroom as well as to why its touching me in places that make me feel bad.

The teacher would always have to call my name loud. It seemed my daydreaming was really distracting me from my classwork. I didn't know what to do. If I was suppose to tell anyone at the time. Back in the 70's in a Hispanic culture there were things you just didn't discuss. So day in and night out. It was a feeling I got used to. I finally realized I probably wasn't the only one going through it.

Well as I continued to go to school. Report cards would come home and me and all of my brothers and sisters feared report card day. That was the day everyone had to stand face to face with Dad and explain why we weren't making straight A's.

He would have the report card in one hand and a leather belt in the other. Our Dad would call us one by one. And if you were a visitor in our home you would witness one or two things. Dad either yelling at us or Dad spanking us in a circle with a leather belt.

With Dad it was either you did good in school or you just wasn't going. Dad always felt if we couldn't pass in school there was no use in wasting good paper when we could just stay home and work. He didn't see the point in any of us going to school if we weren't going to learn. However, all of us sure were relived when he called out the last name. Just meant it would be another six weeks before we faced Dad again. And there was never one 6 weeks that didn't go without one of us crying or one of us explaining to dad, why we were failing school or why we even go.

Sometimes, we would get so scared to show Dad our report cards. Some would sign my Dad's name themselves. I never understood why we were all so scared of my dad. I never asked my Dad for anything I was so scared of him if I wanted money or something from my dad I would usually ask my little sister to ask him for me. That really put a huge wall between us. It was easier for me to go to my mom for everything. I guess it was because I knew what my mom was going through with my dad so I clinged more to my mom, Even if I asked for money it would be my mom that I would go to.

It seemed like all the girls would stay with mom. The boys, well they were pretty much on their own. The older I was getting the more things started to get a worse. The shadow was starting to get a face. The shadow was still coming to my room, still putting his hands in places that hurt. I finally got to where I told one of my sisters Pat what was happening.

My sister would tell me from now on you sleep with me. Which made me feel better, at least I thought. Because at least I know now I would feel safe. Well night came fast and it was time for bed. We got ready for bed. We began to fall asleep.

Well I saw this shadow in our room. Only this time he put his hands on my sister's chest. My sister yelled at him to leave our room. And as fast as he could he ran out of our room. I stayed awake talking to my sister. I later found out my sister would sleep with a knife under her pillow for protection.

I guess she was seeing the shadow as much as I was. She was never really specific or ever given detail on what the shadow would do to her. All she kept telling me was to yell as loud as I could if anyone ever bothered me. At least I knew I wasn't the only one getting visits from the shadow.

So years begin to pass it seemed as if our family was getting smaller. It was either a sister was running away or moving out. There were eight girls in our home. Wouldn't be until my 10th birthday that I realized things a little bit more clearly. You know things that were wrong. I seemed to be getting smarter. There were only 4 of us girls at home now. And we would wake up at 3 am. to make the men their lunches and have Dad's coffee ready before he left to work.

I hated we had to wake up so early. Just meant we got less sleep before school and most of those days we fell asleep in class. Of course, those days we get notes in the mail from the teachers and we had lectures from mom and dad every time we received a note in the mail. Dad would always say, "Watch what's going to happen if you ever get another letter in the mail from any teacher!" So we had to make sure we behaved and not get anymore letters in the mail. Sometimes we walked home so fast just to see if we could get home before the mailman got to our house just in case a letter did get sent to our home.

I didn't understand why our parents were so strict. I mean the kids at my school would brag about going to the movies, or who they would see over there, or the dances they would go to. My mom and dad were so strict that the only thing we ever watched was food getting cooked and laundry getting done.

We were never allowed to date or ever mention boys. Dad always believed if you were old enough to a boyfriend, you were old enough to have a job. Now my oldest sister brought her boyfriend to our house. And we would sit and watch how our dad would scan the guys our sisters dated. He would ask them question like, "Where do you Work?" If the guy would say he didn't work. My dad would want to know how the guy planned on supporting his daughter if he didn't work.

Some guys feared meeting my dad. And well they had good reason. I mean my Dad had 3 shotguns in the hallway as soon as you walked in the front door. My other sisters named Rose ran away from home and my dad didn't get to meet the guy she married. To bad he never did, because maybe my brother-in-law would have never beaten my sister up. I couldn't help but cry. I would wake up early the next day just to walk down the street to go see how my sister was doing. The aftermath wasn't great.

My sister Rose eyes were black, lips were bleeding, eyes were bloodshot red from tears and the beatings. I don't remember a week that didn't go by that my sister Rose didn't get a beating. I hated my brother-in-law for it! Dan worked driving a truck, which I loved. Which meant if he was driving at least he wasn't home beating my sister up. And my sister Rose could get some rest. Rose did everything for Dan. I would watch Rose would cook, clean, iron everyday. And everything had to be perfect. If something was out of order, believe me Dan made sure it wasn't out of order ever again! Rose couldn't go anywhere without someone telling Dan that Rose was riding around or making up lies about her. Just to get her in trouble.

Rose was married to Dan for a long time before reality got the best of her and she finally snapped and killed Dan. I wasn't around when his death occurred. However people said the argument was in the family car. My brother-in-law pulled out a knife on my sister and well the knife accidentally went in my brother-in-law's heart killing him instantly. Whenever I see my sister Rose now, I don't see her as happy as I thought she would be now that she is no longer getting abused domestically.

However I see she is drowning in a lot of hurt from her past. I see she doesn't have any closure. I see Rose continues to carry an unforgivable feeling with her. Cause she never had the chance to ask my brother-in-law to forgive her. Then again Dan never asked her to forgive him either. However two wrongs don't make anything right! My sister still continues to search for that one true love. Like all of us do. I believe my sister has love and control confused.

I believe a lot of people in relationships have it all wrong. Some want to love, some want control, and some want someone to come home too. As for marriage, we would like to believe we know what we are saying ,I do too, and to clear up the marriage part. Some people ask most women, "Why have you chosen to stay with your spouse? Well repeat your marriage vows one day, and it is all right there. "In sickness and in health. For better or for worse." Meaning it doesn't matter what he or she does you are willing to stay married to your partner through the good times and the bad times. Now if you get married and you find out your partner was unfaithful. Well you didn't truly understand you vows. So many couples have said there marriage vows, but it just rolls off their tongues without truly understanding what their vows means. Not saying if a man or woman beats you domestically you're suppose to stay in it. Abuse is never a good way to live. The moment someone starts hitting you or even speaking to you in a way that may be uncomfortable get out of the relationship. Verbal abuse is just as bad as physical abuse. I have been in relationships that were abusive.

I was 16 years old when I ran away from home. I got involved with a guy my dad warned us never to get involved with. I got involved with him out of desperation to get away from all the sexual abuse I was going through at home. Plus my little sister got drunk and we were on foot. We didn't have a ride home and I trusted these guys to take us home. They took us to a motel instead, where my little sister had a one night stand with a guy named Mike. While me and the other guy was in another room, with a knife to my throat and getting raped.

Now I didn't know at the time it was called rape. So I didn't realize this until 8 years later that I in fact got raped that night when I got out of the relationship. I spent 5 years with this guy. He was the first that ever slapped me and gave me a black eye. Once I left him I thought it was over and I would never have to feel that way ever again. Boy was so wrong! Cause the next 8 years was going to be Hell!

I was 21 and I ran away from this guy. I had two little girls with him. I loved my girls so much that I had to decide what was real important to me. My children or my life. Both were important, although I knew if I stayed in the abusive relationship there was no guarantee I would stay alive. Because of the fact my abusive boyfriend would beat me to death. And I would be without my girls either way.

So I decided one day to leave my girls behind with my brother Ed. At least there I new my girls had a chance of being protected and having a good life. So leaving behind my daughters wasn't easy by any means. So I moved on to what I thought was going to be a better life. I moved to a small town called Mexia, Texas. I went to live with a family I thought I knew well. I basically grew up with them. The mother was a pastor.

Well I didn't think I could go wrong with having a relationship with a pastor's son. And again I was wrong. The pastor was so obsessed with herself and her son Lee that she would never hear that her son was getting in a relationship or even getting married. Once the pastor found out I was in a relationship with her son Lee. She tried everything she could to get rid of me.

She tried putting her own son (Lee) down letting me know he was overweight and lazy. Which wasn't the case, all she wanted was to make sure Lee was still giving her his whole paycheck and supporting her. She began finding every little reason for us never be together. She even went as for as saying she wanted to go visit family in my hometown of Cameron, TX.

So she was very nice about it and invited me for the ride. However I didn't know her cruel intentions behind the invite. Well we were on our way to Cameron and well she dropped me off at my sister's house giving me the impression she would be back to pick me up. Why wouldn't she? She was a pastor and why would she lie, so I believed her. So I waited for her while I was with my sister, Rita. It was 3 pm. and it was still early. So I stayed there. My sister Rita was giving me lectures on what I should and shouldn't do. All because Rita was older, she thought she knew better than I did. She probably did too.

However I was at an age where I was going to do what I wanted and how I wanted. I was basically running away from my life and its problems. I didn't know who to talk to. I had no one to confide in at all. Even going through my teenage life I didn't have anyone to tell me about the birds and the bees. My parents were always to busy. My dad thought my mom shouldn't talk to any of us girls about sex or even about our menstrual. He felt we had no business knowing, because it only meant we were going to have sex. My dad was strict on the information we were given. Us, girls were not allowed to even go out. So most of my sisters ran away from home just so they could be with guys they felt they loved.

I don't recall a relationship that any of my sisters had even been in that didn't have some kind of abuse. I just felt that's what everyone went through. Dad taught us when a man hits you, it was because they were showing and proving how much they loved us. So most of my sisters stuck it out and stayed with their men. At least until they wised up and decided they were not going to take it any longer.

Living at home really gave me the wrong impression of love, life, men, and the world. We didn't have a family that encouraged us through school. It was either we made the grade or we stayed home or work to pay bills. There was no time to play. I look back and see what a mess my life was. So much of that could have been prevented. There was no one to protect us girls from any harm we didn't know what it was to feel uncomfortable. Back in the 70's I didn't have any bad thoughts. I mean who did. We were young. I thought little girls were supposed to play with dolls and playhouse. By the time I was 8 years old I was mowing the yards and cooking. Dad was strict for his own reason.

However, after the hours had passed while at my sister's house. I noticed it was getting late and dark. The pastor didn't show up to pick me up. So I called and found out the pastor was in Cameron to drop me off and basically get rid of me so I wouldn't marry (Lee) her son. The pastor was back in Mexia. So I got a ride from a friend of mine on a motor cycle.

I was back in Mexia within a half an hour. By the time the pastor got to her house. She received a call that I was already back in Mexia and I was at her mom's house. Boy! I wasn't prepared for what was going to be a huge shock!

So Lee and I were asleep at her mom's. We heard our bedroom

door bust open! The pastor grabbed me by my arm throwing me out her mom's house. I was in the dark walking around not knowing where to go. Lee was walking around as well. We fell asleep in the park with only a few bucks to get a bite to eat. We survived a cold night before you knew it.

The pastor's mom and dad were riding around looking for us. His grandmother was in tears when she found out we had slept in the park. So she invited us to go back and stay with her. I began to explain I was in fear of the pastor and I didn't want her grabbing me again. She explained it was her house and no one was going to tell her who could live in her home and who couldn't. She was an old fashion church-going woman and very disappointed that her daughter could treat someone this way and continued to call herself a pastor.

So her son and I finally got married. I felt all was going okay. We were living with my husband's grandmother before she let us know they would be moving to Fort Worth. So it was a hint we needed to start looking for our own place which would be difficult. Well I mean he wasn't working and I was on food stamps. So our chance of finding a home was slim to none. However I didn't ever think we would be leaving to move in with his mom. Boy it would be truly Hell on Earth for me.

So before I know it Lee went and asked his mom if we could move in. Of course, Sheila said yes I mean this was her son and Sheila would do anything when it came to her son. So we moved in. Days would pass by and by the time I knew it; I began to notice if we went to the store, the whole family was going. If we wanted to go out and eat, again the whole family was going. It was beginning to feel more like a cult than a family. Seemed like everyone was giving the pastor money, or using money on her.

My dear mother-in-law would use her authority as a pastor as a way to get money from the whole congregation. Well seeing her whole congregation was her own son's and daughter's. Everyone was in competition to be the favorite or should I say her right hand man, when it came to the word of God. My mother-in-law couldn't use anyone if it wasn't her son's or daughter's. I guess she didn't want anybody knowing how her son's and daughters truly were.

As months were passing by and I began going where everyone else was going. I notice our so called pastor was taking things from the store, without paying for it. It was a habit that she tried to hide. However, I had an eye of an eagle. Nothing could get passed me, I just never mentioned it. I knew when to hold my tongue. Even if I did that still was never enough. The only thing that pleased her was if you were giving her a handful of money.

What upsets her most was the fact I was waking up underneath her roof and if I didn't wake up with a smile. She would slap me in my face all because she felt I was in a bad mood. Not that I was. She was just making up excuses to lay her hands on me because she hated the fact I was still around, and because I married her son Lee.

One day her phone rang and it was my mother that called. All I heard was my sister-in-law telling me to pick up the other phone. So I could overhear her conversation with my mom telling my mother-in-law is that she didn't care what she did with me. I was nothing but trouble and I was no good. She didn't want me any longer; those words cut me like a sword.

However my mom didn't know what I was already going through and all my mom did was making it more difficult-than it was already. The abuse began getting worse if it wasn't my mother-in-law beating me up. Her daughter's and son's would take over or they would hold me down just so my mother-in-law could get in a few good punches. I remember one night I had found out I was expecting his second baby. I was only 2 weeks pregnant. Well his older sister was told I called her a dike. This wasn't true. So they all busted in my bedroom began slapping and kicking me before they were told to stop because I was expecting. What was shocking was my mother-in-law wasn't around. She was at the hospital with my father-in-law. When she did found out. She came to our home and hugged me and began to cry. This confused me because she never had a sympathetic bone in her body. Well at least not for me.

At this time I was diagnosed with Epileptic Seizures. Well that wasn't good either because every time I had a seizure anywhere around my mother-in-law. She would tell everyone, "Leave me alone! She just wants attention" and I was left on the floor to go through my seizure all alone with no one to render any aid. I had seizures for years. My mother-in-law would leave me lying on the floor or she would slap me out of it.

She would tell everyone she is plain stupid and expects everyone to feel sorry for her. However, I told her son, "You know one day God will have his vengeance for me and your mom will get her just reward."

Well some years had passed and before you know it we began living in our own home. It was somewhat a relief I didn't have her breathing down my neck. I could at least get some sleep. However, one day another one of her son's came running to our house in a panic. He was telling us his mom had a seizure. I told him well do what she did to me. Slap it out of her, or let her lay there and go through it. It was cruel, but like I told her son. God defends his, and I didn't have to even get my hands dirty.

Well after a couple years I had decided the control, abuse, and not being able to make my own decisions. I mean his mom made all the decisions; pretty much did all the thinking for us. If it wasn't her way it was no way. However, I got really tired of everyone's crap. I even got tired of being the punching bag. So one day I told my husband I was going to the store alone. He said ok. I left never to return, leaving behind my little girl, because I had no where to go.

So I left and went to an abuse shelter near me. If you or a loved one is getting abused Please call your local police station or contact the nearest abuse shelter. Abuse is never worth putting up with. I never understand what abuse was or even realized I was going through it.

It took me years to figure out the physical side of abuse, verbal abuse, even the mental abuse. Somehow everyone of us at one time or another we have been abused. Some of us don't know it or want to realize it because we are blinded by the love or what some of us think is love.

We begin to feel sorry for our abusers. Sometimes we blame ourselves for the abuse. It took me over thirteen years to realize I didn't do anything wrong to ever go through what I went through. I had to really look back at my past and how awful it was. All I could ask myself is "Why?" Everyone I ever went to for help either didn't believe me or tried to come on in a sexual manner.

My mom would take us to church almost 4 days out of the week. My brother, Joe, whom I came to find out later, was the shadow that came in and out of our room every night and touching me. It got so bad he would try to more than fondle me at my young age He was also having oral sex with me. He got so comfortable with what he was doing to us.

Well he would go to the church we went to and he began to brag to our cousins that went there. By the time I knew it, even our cousins were making sexual advances to us as well. We couldn't get around our own family; they all had sick, twisted thoughts. Seemed like something that went from generation to generation. I would always ask my mom about it. I just couldn't build up the courage to do it.

I was 38 years old when I and my little sister began talking on the phone one day. And out of the blue she was telling my older sister, Dianna told my mom why a lot of us girls resented her. It was because as a mother, my mom was suppose to protect us from anything and when we went to her and told her what was happening. She wouldn't listen; mom would always say we were crazy.

Then before my sister Dianna's conversation with my mom was over. My mom admitted she knew of all the sexual abuse we were going through. She claimed she loved my dad too much to leave or do anything. So we were left for the wolves sort of speak. When I found out I was in shock and began to feel hate for my mother. There are times when I feel I should say something to her however I don't. I was raised to respect my elders and always respect my mother. I feel there is a higher power I feel that will deal with her.

However when I was 16 yrs old I did file charges against my brother. I moved out of our home. My mom had all my brothers, sisters, and in-laws take part in destroying the home that all the abuse took place in. They didn't want the police to go into our home and find all the evidence. I go by there every once in awhile and all that's there is an empty parking lot.

It was a home that should have been destroyed way before we even moved in. Our parents made us live in a way no child should ever have to live. Now that I am a mother of 4 children, I raise my kids to have respect for themselves and each other as well as there bodies. If for any reason anyone touches them to where they feel uncomfortable they are to tell me at once. Even if it's an advance made by someone I want my kids to know they can come to me and talk to me about anything.

I don't want my kids to fear me. I don't want them to feel they can't talk to me. There are days we go riding and we talk about there day at school. We try to be open about all subjects. As a parent I have to look at my children and ask myself. Do my children feel comfortable talking to me? Is there anything I feel they can't talk to me about? If I feel there is a yes to any of these questions I have to keep talking to my children and make sure there is no doubt that they can't come to me for anything.

My advice to all of you mothers is asking yourself all those questions. Really get personal with your children; you will be surprised what your children know. We can raise our kids to the best of our abilities. However we can't protect them from what they learn from outside our homes. However what they learn from the world is not our fault. There are kids that are just trying to fit in.

However it's our job to really see what and who our kids know. There are times that I just ride around in my town and I see young kids walking alone. I say to myself, "I wonder if there parents know where there at?" or "Why is a kid that young walking all alone?" At times I want to stop and ask if there parents know where there at? At times we parents allow our kids to walk out of our homes not knowing who there connected with.

When it comes to the outside world we allow our kids to walk outside our home. We are basically saying we trust that the world won't hurt our kids or introduce them to drugs or even hurt them in a sexual way. However the world doesn't give us a written contract promising a thing. I have a 13 year old son and when he asked me, "If he could walk home from school?" I wasn't comfortable I would ask questions like, "Why do you want to walk home? Who are you going to be walking with?"

He would walk home but I would supervise while he was walking. Just to make sure he wasn't smoking or making sure nobody wasn't trying to pressure him into doing something he has no business doing. I trying to do what wasn't done with me when I was growing up. There were twelve of us in my family. Once we were able to walk on our own. There were things that my mom tried to teach us. It wasn't the teaching she needed to know.

It was the protection I feel if my mom would have protected us the way she should have the world would have never got a hold of us. I remember going to school when I was in the 7th grade and one of my friends name was Sonia. She was in a relationship with a guy and was in love with that guy so much. He began grabbing her and telling her who she could and could not speak to. He began pulling her by her hair.

I mean he was just a school boyfriend I figured well she could dump the guy and move on to better things. Well about five years later I found out Sonia married the guy. She lived unhappy for at least four years. I wondered why she lived that way; however with the relationship I was in I understood.

I felt a guy that beat, slapped or mistreated me. Well the more he loved me; at least that is what my mom made me believe. Teenage girls often believe the moment a guy says they love them they drown hearing those words. Usually it is the girls that don't hear those words very often. So they cling on to the first person that makes them believe it, and when the abuse begins its hard for them to leave it because there afraid no one will ever give it to them ever again

It is easy for a guy to make a woman or teenage girl feel there worthless and never amount to anything. At times women and teenage girls allow those words to compute in our minds. We allow it to break our souls and our minds and weaken us so bad to where we believe it! So therefore we choose to stay where we are at, and we feel the search for anyone better is over!

However ladies and teenage girls listen up! Don't ever allow a man to make you believe that you're not worth being respected or treated any less than a queen. Were like porcelain dolls. We need to be treated like were fragile, very special, and with tender-loving care.

We women have been doing the cooking, cleaning, and raising our children since the beginning of time and we still continue to do. So why should we allow a man to treat us any less than were really worth. Ask yourself how many times does your partner put you down or insult you compared to many compliments he gives you? Teenage girls, does your boyfriend respect you all the time or sometimes?

Back in the days men open car doors for a young lady. They held hands and walked, talked, or even went to the movies. They even made sure young ladies were brought home at a decent hour. Men had a respect for parents and elders. It was always yes ma'am or yes sir. Not this disrespect all these teenagers have nowadays with there fowl language which shows no respect. Everyone has forgotten what true love is. Back in my day if I disrespected my parents there was leather belt waiting to put me in my place.

Now I'm not saying use a leather belt on your children. Our generation has quit teaching, talking, and getting personal with our kids. And then when we get a call that is about your child is using profanity we are in shock all of a sudden. When we shouldn't be blame anyone but ourselves for not talking to our kids. Some parents have a fear of finding out what our kids know. I was scared at first because I didn't want to know my kids were growing up or becoming adults. I thought my kids didn't need to know. But if they didn't someone else would make sure they did find out. So I had to start taking to them. At times my son was somewhat embarrassed to talk about relationships or sex.

However I tell him I don't ever want him to feel he can't talk to me about anything and everything. When I was growing up and I got to the age where I was getting interested in boys. Well that's all I could do. I couldn't go out or even go to friend's house. Not the way teenagers do nowadays I mean back in my school days it bothered me to see some girls walk around with hickeys, or even hear conversation about what they did the night before.

It also bothered me that the girls would get flowers or homecoming mums from there boyfriends delivered to the school. I use to think it must be real cool to get something from a boyfriend. I use to think you would have to get a passing grade in school to get a boyfriend. And for me to get a passing grade in school was a joke. I never studied for anything I really just didn't put any effort into school. I didn't see the point. I felt it was a rich mans world and you were never going to amount to anything, without having money or a brick home. Teachers treated students according to wealth, grades and if you were part of an athletic team.

Somehow teachers had to know a student was going to amount to something or making an effort to get somewhere in life before you could get any help or attention. I was from a poor broken down home; a person that was living in the hood. I was real cautious about who I hung around with. I got along pretty well with others. It was hard because there were those who would always needed to be the center of attention and tease me about my family and how we lived.

I hated it and I would always go home and ask my mom. "Why we had to live in this house?", that I felt was only made for fire wood. All she would say is, "Be grateful for having a roof over your head. Cause there is people that don't even have that." I never felt mom really did there best for us. I felt we had to settle for less so they could have better than we did. Today my mom lives in a huge home. And I ask myself why she couldn't have us living in a home like that growing up. Now that all my brothers and sisters are grown and we all have our own lives.

My mom is living great, better than we ever did. She has a nice car, while she drove us in a broken down car. It feels like she couldn't wait for any of us to leave home. So she could have what we deserved. We just never received it. I teach my kids to manage there money. I'm not rich by any means. However I do my best to get my kids what they need. I have to make them understand there are times we can't all get what we want.

There are times when we can't have steak and we have to settle for stew. I would love for my children to have the fine things in life. However it is almost impossible. I just try that much harder and add more determination and extra amount of love. Before you know it you have it all and it all boils down to family. I want my kids to be strong and dependent.

Now I'm not saying that women or teenage girls can't be as bad as a man. Cause we can be. I'm sure there are teenage boys that have gone through some kind of abuse. We just don't know how to handle it, what to say, or who and who not to say it too. Why? It all comes to the fear. We think about what's going to happen to us if our abusers find out we told. What will he or she do to us? Will we go to jail or a shelter? Where would we stay?

Sometimes, if not most of the time we are wrong about not having money because without money you can't really get too far. It was hard to leave my abuser; I didn't have a dime to my name. Sure I had family but no one in my family would take me in. I mean I reported my older brother to the law enforcement and because I did that. Everyone turn there back on me. I did what I felt was right not only for me but for all of my sisters. I guess because no one ever stood up to my mom and dad, everyone was in shock. I didn't ask my sisters how they felt after I reported the abuse. It seems like everyone grew up silent again.

I remember when I made the report. My little sister Nancy called me told me to lock my doors. I asked why? Nancy said "Dad is drunk and he has a loaded shot gun and he is looking for you!" I remember I was so scared and I didn't know if he wanted to kill me because he felt betrayed or because he could no longer have a sex toy for his son any longer. I myself until this day still don't understand why. As for my brother well I have not spoken to him since I left home at the age of 16. I saw him maybe once. He walks around with his head in his chest and guilt that I'm sure eats him up every time he sees me. I don't see how my sisters get around him. Now that he is married I'm afraid for his wife. One day he will have a daughter and I hate to imagine what if he would put his daughter through it too.

I never met his wife. I've seen her and when I did I hated her because she married someone I wouldn't trust with my life. My older sister tried to encourage her to speak to me. I told my sister I would not advise that. My first question would be to her. "Of all the men in the world, why him?" And I would walk away. They finally had a baby together. Thank God it was a boy. God Sure knows where to put his angels. It like this world is a huge garden and God knows where to plant each tree.

I spoke to my sister Nancy and I asked her how she felt once she found out my mom knew about the sexual abuse going on in the house? Nancy replied, "Well I was not only upset, I despised our mother. I didn't speak to mom for awhile." It got so bad that I know all of us as brothers and sisters could get together for the holidays if our mother would have protected us. Which my sisters were right we don't gather together for Christmas or Thanksgiving all at once.

There is still so much hate, hurt, and animosity towards each other we as little sisters felt our older sisters should have taken us with them when they ran away from home. I don't know if they ever worried about us once when they were gone. I believe I was the one that got the worst of it, when my brother began having oral sex with me by the time I was ten years old.

We went from being born straight to the kitchen to relationships. Our childhood wasn't normal at all. I don't know what a normal childhood is like. I don't know even know what it had been like to go to the prom or even having some guy buy me a homecoming mum. I wish I knew though.

Now as a mother since my daughter had her prom I made sure she went. I allowed her date. Her boyfriend got her a mum and a gift for every occasion, he made her feel special. Parents need to explain to there teenage daughters that a guy should make them feel special. Not like property or a servant but as an equal.

There are some guys who want to use a girl to get what they want. They can easily persuade a girl into believing anything if a girl is weak-minded. Especially, when your daughter gets her first boyfriend. Some boys prey on the innocent girls. So to all mothers teach your young teenage girls as well as yourself to be strong minded and be firm when having to say no! That's what it is. Teach your young teenagers not to feel they have to fear anyone for any reason. If they need to tell you something good or bad they can always trust going to mom or dad.

Sometimes we ourselves make mistakes as parents and because we are parents we don't even realize it what I mean by this is we have a tendency to yell at our kids instead of talking to them calmly. At times our conversation with our kids begins calmly, and then all of a sudden we are having a yelling match. I know when I was a teenage girl growing up the last thing I ever did was yell at my mom and dad. I would get slapped down in a hurry.

However I always stayed cautious because of the fear I had towards my dad. And because of that fear I could never go to my dad for a thing. I grew up knowing me and my sisters and brothers we couldn't have a family relationship cause it was ruined by there own sick twisted acts. Not one of us could ever have mother-daughter conversation with our mom. We learned just by doing if we got pregnant, well it was like how? I still kept trying to figure it out. At least until I went to Planned Parenthood. And have someone I didn't even know explain it to me. I was somewhat grateful at least I knew I could prevent getting pregnant.

I'm 40 years old and I still don't know a lot of things about the female body. I still get uncomfortable when a doctor does pap smears on me. However I do them regularly to make sure I'm still in perfect health. To all mothers there is nothing wrong with getting your young teenage girl to a Planned Parenthood sometimes young teens cant go to us mothers and say, "Mom I feel I might be sexually active." because as mothers we don't want to know our girls are growing up and they're maturing. We don't want to know that soon one day our kids will be leaving home. We want our kids to stay innocent all our lives.

However newsflash! We all grow up and we all move on. Sometimes when our kids do things we need to reflect on our own lives compared to the things and mistakes our own kids make. It won't surprise you that we didn't do everything perfect either when we were teens. Everyone needs somebody sometimes. However some people like me aren't that fortunate, before you know it there learning from the world out of fear. They debate on how the mother or father is going to react if we ask them about sex or protection. We parents teach our kids what we were taught I had to think about that. Because everything I was taught wasn't always right.

I raised my children different from what I was raised by my parents. It is a generation thing its like saying teach what you have been taught which wasn't always right. I didn't want to make the same mistakes my parents made with me. Now I'm not saying everything they taught me was wrong. However sometimes we parents need to break some cycles. We can't help what we ourselves were taught it's like a student when he or she begins Pre-K at school they begin to learn there basics, ABC's, and 123's. Why because that's what the teachers are passing down what he or she was taught by someone else.

One day when you are sitting down get a sheet of paper. Write at the top of the paper the number 24 real big. Now begin to write what exactly you do each hour of the day then when your done writing down what you do for the first 24hours take a good look at it and see where your kids fit in and how much time you spend talking to them. You will be amazed sometimes we parents are busy with work, maintaining a home, cooking, and cleaning before you know it the whole day is gone.

It seems like even when we have to go to work for 8 hours a day. We get off work to go home to more work. Seems like there is never enough time in the day and before you know it another day and conversations with our kids are gone. Our kids keep getting older then you turn around and your own kids are telling you things you didn't realize he or she knew then you wonder where there getting their information from or who.

I have a 13 year old son, I didn't have the slightest idea he new how to play a guitar. We were walking one day and he began to tell me how he enjoyed playing the guitar. I began to ask him "How did he learn to play a guitar?" Because I know I didn't teach him. I'm his mother and I don't know how to play any instruments at all. He said "Mom I take music class at school." So just to see if he was saying was the truth. I put a guitar in his hand and he began to play a tune I began to cry. Because I didn't realize how much I was missing out. However it taught me a lesson. Take time to talk and teach my kids or someone else will. If we allow someone else to teach them there way and we ourselves won't like it.

My first time speaking to my son about sex began with my son telling me about a video he looked at when he was at school. I asked him "What it was about?" He told me it was about puberty he said "It was embarrassing to talk about." I told him I'm your mother. He feels he should talk to a man about it I asked him "Do you know what a condom was?" He is 13 and interested in girls so felt it was time. He said "No". I began to tell him what it was and how it was used however it hurt me that he didn't want me speaking to him about the subject so I asked him questions about girls, sex, and boys?

And his views are so wrong. Basically what I'm saying is this. We don't get into the heart of things when it comes to our children. Get personal with them you will be surprised what all your young teens know and don't know nowadays. At times I can be going to the store just to go shopping. I see couples together with there kids and I say to myself why couldn't my family be that close. Why any of our brothers couldn't love us like brother should love sisters. I still don't know why any of this happened, why no one tried to stop it. I also wondered how many family members knew it was happening and who started It.? Many of my questions will never be answered.

It really got so bad my older my brother was starting to have oral sex with me. Tears would roll down my face. Once I told my mom and dad. All I heard my dad say was "Get rid of her she is crazy!" So my mom called a lady and had her pick me up. I stayed with her for two or three months until the summer. I didn't understand why they were getting rid of me for telling the truth. I hated being away from home because my little sister was the only one left and I knew she was going threw it now.

She couldn't go anywhere because my brother would bribe her into having sex with him for just leaving the house without asking dad. I later found out both my mom and dad knew all this sexual abuse was going on with all of us. I didn't know how to respond once I found out! I wanted to hate my father. But I was never close to him any how.

As for my mom I was very close to her and the very thought of her betraying us the way she did, had me in shock! I couldn't believe it at all.

I felt the only person I trusted to go to all this time I could no longer go to. I had questions of who my dad and mom really were. Were we all adopted? Because for all eight of us to go through such a horrible life with no one to ever protect us. These couldn't be our real parents.

My mother would have protected us some how. However I found out my mom wouldn't do anything because she never wanted to lose my dad for some reason. However we continued to get older and the older we got the more questions we had. However we never received responses. I remember my little sister telling me what my dad told her. "We went through this because God was punishing us girls for not listening." I hated our lives if it wasn't our brothers sexually abusing us it was a cousin. However the family love was confusing. We didn't know who to hug who to say we love you to without it being misinterpreted.

Until this day we still can't make since out of any of it! It was a mess. I remember when my little sister thought about ending her life because of it! I Thank God she didn't go through with it! So now all we can do with all the unanswered questions is continue on with life without anyone explaining to us why? Our ordeal has made us all very strong. We know now we don't have to take anything a man gives us.

When a person is wrong they need to know it! Make it know at all times if a man or woman is making you feel uncomfortable! Let them be aware they are in a Red Zone and it is making you feel uncomfortable. Always remember sexual abuse is out there! And it shouldn't be taken lightly. If your child is telling you that someone is making them feel uncomfortable even if its family or friend.

Listen! Once again, if you or anybody is a victim of abuse, whether it is physically, emotionally, mentally, or sexually. Call your local Police station or nearest abuse shelter.

After I grew up moved and Ran away in the year 2000 I met a guy I thought was a guy I could trust without a doubt His name was Tony and the first time he hugged me it felt as if I was floating on clouds and man it was something.

For the first time I actually slept through the night in his house without worrying about who was going to sneak in my room or was anyone going to watch me take a shower through the window, I was scared when I met him. I had been through so much abuse I couldn't trust. It was very hard. I was having Flash backs of my times at home.

Seem liked every time I was going to take a shower I would see visions of my brother watching me & I would freak out so bad. I would run out side the shower completely naked just to lock myself in my bedroom and cover up in fear. Tony always had a way of reassuring me no one would ever hurt me again.

Even though Tony told me it was real hard to believe so slowly but surely I began living my life with Tony. He seemed harmless. Myself and my ex husband use to live by Tony we were his neighbors. We became friends and nothing more. At least that's what I new. Somehow my ex-husband felt there was more than friendship between me & Tony for some reason.

So one day I told my ex-husband I was leaving him, That I couldn't live with his family abusing me mistreating me. I was going to move back to my mom's house. He didn't know that. So he took in upon himself to tell Tony That I thought he could make me happy. Before I knew it my ex-husband was moving my things in Tony's house so that's where I stayed.

After that Tony asked me too marry him. I said yes of course. It all seemed like a dream. That a man could be this loving and sweet. But before I new it I began to see a change in Tony after a year of being married to him, he became distance. I didn't know why I felt this way. Me as a wife I thought I was doing all the right things especially in the bedroom. I didn't think I would ever find myself asking questions like why is he distant. What am I doing wrong? At least not with Tony, and seeing we just got married.

However things didn't go right on our wedding day either. I mean we were late to our wedding, there was no Honeymoon & even after we were married we didn't eat the first bite of our cake like they do traditionally.

Well we were only married for 15 months before I had to go to a state prison for a government tampering charge that had caught up with me. So I had to sit 18 months in the prison. I spent my whole time writing and begging Tony to come and visit or at least write. You would think knowing his newlywed wife was in prison he would visit on a regular basis. However the months got longer, weeks felt like forever. Until I received a letter from my husband's daughter explaining my husband had another woman living with him.

I couldn't help but cry while I was in prison. I wouldn't eat I was so angry I began getting into trouble not wanting to do anything. I was getting depressed until I got out October 15, 2003. When I was released I was eager to get home. Smelling the flower & actually eating real food. I finally got home. And it didn't seem like home at all. The grass was so tall we passed the house. I entered the house & it felt so cold like I was in a cave.

We walked through the house & I got to the kitchen where the floor was covered in grease so thick a person could cut it with a knife. I kept walking through the house till I got to my kids bedroom. I was in shocked. All 383 letters I ever wrote my husband all in one room all boxed up. Not one letter was ever read. It hurt me to my soul knowing while I was in prison pouring my heart and soul to him, he never read one of my letters, so he never new what I went through when I was in there.

Everyone asked me why did I stay? Well I stayed because I remembered my wedding vows In sickness and in health For Better or worse. To me it didn't matter how wrong he was it was my love and God that help me to overcome those difficult times. I thought things were going to be fine once I was home. Then there were phone calls coming to the house. It was another woman & when I asked my husband who she was he claimed it was a woman he was working for. So I let it go. So I kept doing my choirs at home.

I don't know why, but something asked me to look in the closet in the room. I was going through shirt pockets & I came upon a diamond bracelet. I put it on and once Tony had seen it & asked where did I find it. When I asked who it belong to Tony said it belong to a friend of his. I told him to return it & he said he didn't know where she lived. But yet the bracelet disappeared. I knew he knew where she lived. Her name was Jennifer another female he was seeing. All his infidelity traits began to show. It was hard but difficult. We also got passed it because she had moved away.

Once I was home for awhile I got me a job at a local hamburger joint. I had to do something to keep my mind off Tony. Even when I was at work he was still seeing other women. This time I found out he was trying to sleep with our next door neighbor. If her husband wouldn't have told me I would have never known. So I had a friend of mine come pick me up and take me out on dates just to get back at him. We dated for 4 months.

He would pick me up when Tony was home & I thought it would make him a little jealous but my husband never reacted at all. To what I was doing. I told Tony it is not normal for a man not to react when his wife is seeing another man. I told Tony he was made of Stone. Seemed like nothing ever affected him the way it would a normal man.

We moved on to continue our lives I quit working to take care of his dad & grandsons. While he began to work. He found a good job so I thought it was good, Seemed he was getting home at a descent hour at least for awhile. Then all of a sudden his hours were getting longer & he began treating me different. Talking to me as if he was angry & I not knowing what I did wrong. I was starting to feel he was seeing someone else, but I just couldn't prove it.

But one day I drove up to my house & there was a guy standing in my yard & asked if I knew Tony Perez I said yes he was my husband & before the man could say anything. I told him; let me guess My Husband is having an affair with your wife? He asked how I knew. I said he has done this so many times its nothing new. The guy asked if I would go visit his wife & I asked why? So I can ask her why she is sleeping with my husband when she has a husband.

He gave me her address & I went along with my step-daughter. When the woman came out of her apartment I was shocked & couldn't help but laugh. The lady was 200 lbs heavier, ugly like you couldn't believe it really doesn't take Tony long to get busy he tries to make me believe that he is not looking for another woman. Yet, he is such a big hurry to get me out of the house.

For the last two weeks he had been getting us burritos down the street. Every time he sees a female that catches his attention he goes to the same store over & over. Just to see if she will give him the time of day He knows what to say to me just to get me to forget about what he is doing. I know he no longer loves me he only sleeps with me because he feels he has to. I'm ashamed to be his wife sometimes.

I compare myself to every woman & just knowing I will never have him love me the way he loved them, well it hurts to my soul. I always felt I had to prove myself, when I wasn't the one that did any wrong. He always thought every woman needs him and they don't cause if they did there would be a line at the door now. At times I feel my shadow left my side That I no longer have a partner, I feel at times I am difficult for anyone to ever be happy with.

I can no longer stick around with a man that hurts me and does things and has nothing but disrespect towards a woman. Women in today's society feel they have to have a man & a man feels they have to have a woman. All a woman wants is to have some real love, respect& have faithful partner just like a man does as well. Women want to be considered equals when it comes to a relationship. Not a man that comes home from work telling us what we need to do or how we need to feel or do our thinking for us. All because a man want us to feel comfortable with what they are doing even if it hurt us to our souls.

There are some women who want just to go out and have a good time with there husbands or boyfriends. However if were not getting money to pay just the bills, well ladies half of the time were not given any money unless we work for it ourselves. Now don't get me wrong men want to be treated just as well as we do. However they want to be treated where they want us ladies to except them side dishes they have or would like to have. I hate there is so many affairs being taken place. It's all over TVs, the newspapers, and the magazines.

I mean why get married if you are not completely done with dating or going out? Why get married just to hurt someone who you just said your marriage vows to? Before you go outside your marriage and begin to have affairs. Ask yourself this. What did my mate or spouse deserve for me to treat him or her that way? Or why am I making this choice? We know this world is not perfect and never will be. The world is difficult enough without grown adults misbehaving in ways that are inappropriate and hurting people they trusted there lives and children with.

My life has had so many traumatic experiences, that it seems I have been forced to except this all the time. Because anytime I have allowed my mind to let go of one bad experience another bad experience happens. Its like planting a flower, You know its going to need water to grow& it will keep growing until the season passes& then it will die, until the new season comes again& it will the same routine but a different flower. And if it is a plant or flower you didn't like well its best not to plant the same one. If there is something you don't like about your life, don't complain to others about it, just change it!

Once I ran away from home it wasn't easy allowing a man to have sex with me. I would have all sorts of flash backs. With all 3 of my relationships only 2 I felt I was being raped. If I said I didn't feel like having sex with these men they would force themselves on me holding my mouth shut while they had there way with me. I don't think I ever knew what it was like to actually have a man really fall in love with me I was so busy running and chasing guys I always chose the wrong ones .

I believe it was because I was seeking more shelter then anything, However I guess that shelter came at a heavy price. I still talk to these men I was involved with &now they wish they still had me. There left with only the guilt of what they did to me and how they treated me & the apologies come sometimes. They only treated me the way they were treated. I see my kids as they are getting older & I have one daughter that is going through the domestic violence she has come home two times during her ordeal & I can only pray one day she comes home to stay permanent.

I cry to see that she got caught in the same cycle I was in; I pray she breaks it before it's too late. Our Children are our future When I seen that my daughter was going through what I went through I was shocked, because that was not the kind of life I ever wanted her to live. When I left my daughter behind I did it because I was battling abuse with her dad as well. I was 16 not old enough to raise a baby , I didn't know what I was doing , I didn't know how to cook ,clean ,iron or even wash. I wasn't dumb... I was just young & wasn't taught everything when it came to being a young girl.

I felt someone put the world in the palm of my hands & said here is the world now u takes care of it! I couldn't go to my family they didn't like the daddy of my kids , so I never asked them for help until I left him & even then they couldn't help. However I lived with my 2 grown girls sometimes reminding me of the fact I was never there, I didn't leave because I didn't want my girls. I left for the safety of my life.

I loved and adored my girls, my girls will never know how many sleepless night I had worrying about them, I had little contact with them. However I kept hearing they were fine. I didn't know where they moved to. Seem like every time I would even ask seemed no one knew. Until I was invited to my oldest daughters' graduation I was shocked to even receive one. But when I did it was a huge honor to go to. I went & for the first time in almost 17 years, I had seen my daughter.

She was beautiful standing in her graduation gown. In the back of my mind I said, "I wondered if I would have been in the picture would she had graduated?" I didn't know. But I was sure glad she accomplished something good in her life regardless of whether I was there or not.

She had grown so much I seen in her eye that anything I had to say to her well she wasn't hearing. I didn't blame her however they will never know or understand what I had endure the five years I was with their father. But now that there older & they were raised by there father I would think they would understand by now. However my oldest daughter will be getting married she is a Christian. She loves god with all her heart & everyone knows you can't go wrong with God.

I knew I took my eyes off the only spiritual father I had know all my life. I was telling my other daughter yesterday, that a lot of our misery is because its our own faults. It's because of our selfish acts for one and that we couldn't wait on God to begin with. God doesn't want us to suffer, we do things because we refuse to wait on the blessing's he has for us. We think well, God isn't doing it fast enough. Why do we rush our life and God's plans,we began to cry, complain an be miserable. Why because we didn't give God a chance! Don't complain we are our own worse enemies. We have no one to blame but ourselves for our lives and failures ,we can either wait on God's plan or we can just keep doing what we are doing. Messing our lives up by are own selfish decisions. It's up to us how we want our lives to be, remember Its God that has the first and last say so in our lives. I look back on my life,there's a lot I wish of could have done different, I wanted to graduate, go to college ,become a beautician, work for a hair salon or become a great cook. Now I can cook average food not any New York style like the great chefs cook. However I go with what I know & just keep living. When I was going through my childhood abuse I felt that had a lot to do with my failures at school. I didn't have anyone that was listening. I remember trying to draw pictures of what was going on at home for my teachers. But teachers never paid attention to that kind of thing. I guess they never figured anyone went through that. Today I open up a news paper, there was article speaking about a teacher that was arrest for sex acts with a child at the age of 5,they allowed him to go back to teaching. That kind of thing angers me to know even in school a child can't be protected. When a child goes through it at home,then they have to go to school to endure the same thing u know the world has to be insane. When I got into junior high school ,I was getting to that age where I was getting interested in boys ,like I said earlier in my book that was a big no at home. I would dress in ways my mom didn't approve of .My sister an I would sneak certain shirts in our purses just so we could wear them at school, we would flirt with the boys at school. However boys didn't seem interested in us, I guess we were not blonde or rich. I always felt unattractive when it came to the way I looked, I didn't have the straight teeth wavy long hair. Didn't have an expensive car to go to school in. we were poor,an boy it was an embarrassing times. When I was growing up clothing didn't matter,In school it seem like it mattered to everyone else. Now days it's the Name brand if you're wearing anything from the dollar store . I never knew where my mom bought our clothes from. Just to know most of it was given to us by friends or family. Mostly a lot of hand me downs, if it fit ;it fit if it didn't well we had to make it fit somehow. Sometime our pants were to short or not long enough. My mom and dad never knew of any humiliation we went through at school, or the embarrassment .If they did ,they sure seemed to hide it well. I don't know if my moms and dad's friend asked them about the house we lived in. I keep going back in fourth in my book about things because it takes me back to certain times. Example I remember the time I walked in my brother's room. I was alone in the upstairs room ,he wasn't home ,as I began to look around I looked into his closet. Inside a closet u would think there would be you're basic shirts hanging up or shoes right? Well there wasn't anything hanging, there were two huge boxes. As I opened up the boxes to see what they had in them all I could see were magazines, I didn't know what type of magazines they were. As I began to flip through them , I saw nothing but pictures and photos of nude women. I thought ,what's my brother doing with such books. I looked around an notice huge holes in his bedroom wall. I got a chair and put it by the wall just so I could stand on it to see what he could possibly seeing through theses walls, I got on the chair stood on the very tips of my toes, looked through the hole. I was scared ,I noticed he could see everything in our bedroom. Just to make sure I had to hurry to the other side of the hole to make sure what I was seeing was true. So I put the same chair in our room an stood on the tips of my toes one more time, only this time I could see everything in his room. I heard a car door shut, I didn't know who it was so i had to hurry and get the chair back down stairs to the dinning room ,before my brother seen it was missing or that I had been in his room. I waited to get one of my sisters alone to let them know they had to cover the holes in the walls, we were being watched as we would change or get dressed . I told my sister Patricia about it one day, she said your lying ,I said no ,I told her to take a look through the hole in the wall. I got on my knees just so my sister could stand on my back just so she could look through the hole. She was in shock ,So she told me get some wet toilet paper or some black tape and cover the holes. I Thought it would work, but every time we would go back to the room t,here was a fresh holes just made. Seemed like every where we got dressed ,there was always someone looking at us change or take a bath. I even remembered one day ,I was playing outside the house ,an was running around the house and well we rarely went to the back of the house. I noticed a bucket turned upside down, it was below the bathroom window. I stood on top of it to see what I could see I noticed it was the restroom. I ran into the house once again. I told my sister Patricia to come with me, she asked what I wanted. I said just come with me I have to show you something ,took her to the back of the house an told her someone is standing on this bucket, watching us take a bath. She said you're crazy, I told her stand on the bucket and tell me what u see. Patricia stood on the bucket to take a look, I asked her what we do. She told me u don't know for sure. Then I told her when I take a shower I heard things outside like someone fell down, I never paid much attention until I seen the bucket outside. She told me ,tell u what when we shower we need to do it as soon as we get home. The guys are at work, if one of us is taking a shower when the guys get home you or Nancy go to the back of the house, make sure no one is outside in the back. However that wasn't going to matter because we found out later they were even getting into the roof of the restroom, just to watch us take baths. Seems as there was no privacy at all. I don't understand what they even got out of watching us, I don't know why anyone didn't suspect anything. I always wanted to ask my dad why he allowed the things that happen to us happen. I never would really get that chance my dad had died .when I began to speak to him 13 years after never seeing him, he had passed. I loved my dad ,but we never had a dad a daughter relationship with him,where I could go to him about anything. I feared my dad in the worst way. It's Sad to say but it's true. Seemed everyone began to die after my dad passed, had two cousins die after him a uncle as well as a father-in-law all within a year's time. I always wondered why my dad never apologized or if he even regrets the life he felt he didn't build for us or the way he was never there? If he didn't have any regrets at all well he never admitted to it, if he did he never admitted it to me. I wondered if he ever talked to my brothers about the things they were doing to us. Was he encouraging them to do it or was he upset at them. I never knew of any conversations my dad had with anyone. Other than my brother-in-law and that was usually about cars or yard work. Other than not recalling any of that even sounding like he ever cared about us, well at least about us girls. Made me wonder if he regret us ever being born. I will never understand what we did so wrong that our lives couldn't have been better. There was some times that my mom and dad as well as our brothers were not home and it was all of us girl. Seemed like those were the days we were at ease and didn't have to feel uncomfortable , if we wanted to wear shorts, we couldn't without someone looking at us in some sick disgusting way. When I seen all this happening I would make sure I wore long shirts that went to my knees just to make sure I wasn't showing any skin. Its like in today's world Women cat wear a low cut shirt & even speak to a man without them looking down there shirts . We couldn't even wear tight paints without a man looking at our behinds. when we meet guys is it our looks, personality, our bodies or is it our souls. When we go on these dating experiences what is it that we are seeking. If its perfection that we will never have Unless God gives it to us. Are we just seeking someone just to pass the time with or something more? I mean when we women and men sleep with someone is it just for the couple of minutes of pleasure, Is it they believe they can get better out of a total stranger. Women sometimes can be as faithful as they can be, I'm not saying a man can't be faithful because there are some out there. But what makes the faithful ones be unfaithful is it the sure fact there partner is already being unfaithful you sure can't expect the person your married to just sit back an watch you hurt him or her. There either going to do it as well or going to move on. I dealt with this for 9 yrs and I continue to be faithful, however there are thoughts that go through my mind wondering should

I continue to be faithful or should I join the sinners of the world and do as everyone does. I know that if I did this it would be because there are things my mate no longer does. I miss the passion , I miss someone holding me , caressing me. It's the things a man or a woman begins to forget about in there marriage that allows them to go off looking and searching. It's the absence that makes us look in a direction other than the direction that is right in front of us. Therefore we hurt the one that stood by us through it all. At times some partners are willing to forgive, however there are those that wouldn't give you another chance for all the money in the world. So before we become that unfaithful person think about that wife or husband or child that is at home shedding tears with a broken hearts, wondering why you hurt him the way you did. Think about that when you're sleeping with someone. what is it that you're really taking home to your family besides the heart ache and pain because you may just be taking a little more than you really bargained for. I look at my grandsons and I watch as my daughters raise there sons I ask myself, did I do all the right things in directing my kids. I give them all the right advice will my grandsons get all the proper advice and direction in life that they deserve. I don't want my children to know pain. But the world is made up of lots of things, we may not like all the things the world is made of. But one thing is for sure we can't stop the world from ever going around. If we don't protect our kids who will? At times I walk through my daughter's high school, have never seen so much making out in public than I have in this school. It's like it doesn't matter to today's students. There are even same sex relationships in my daughters school a lot of things that were not allowed in the schools I went to. We were not allowed to walk, holding a boy or girls hand, we were not allowed to kiss on each other. Today it's like one huge orgy .I wait to see how teachers react to this behavior and I haven't seen a reaction yet. I remember one day I was talking to a teacher at this school and we were in the hall way . I had seen two students outside in front of the school practically kissing on the sidewalk. I told the teacher interesting this must be a new extra curricular activity the school must have ,the teacher looked at the students then looked at me an smiled. What is being taught at these schools now days is beyond me. There are some teachers there that mean business and do 'take certain things to lightly some go by the book and well others do what they feel is best. I'm just trying to figure out how the students got into the same sex thing. Now don't get me wrong everyone has the right to love who they choose. But at such an early age, where do they receive all there information from? Is it from family, friends or is it a magazine. Why do they do what they are doing? Is it from the lack of love and attention ,our parents never gave? I sometimes see teens that walk around with a rude attitude with no respect at all. And have this I don't care attitude on them. As if the world owes them something. What is it a teenagers seeks well think about the things that ourselves as a young teens or a child wasn't getting when we were home What did we look for? What were we trying to gain? I know I wanted a great reputation however, because of what I didn't have I was treated like I was beneath the students and friends I wish I had. I use to envy students that lived in a brick home. When I take my daughter to school an I see her reputation is on the line because of what I don't have or the fancy clothes she doesn't wear. I do my best to drive something nice just so my kids won't be made fun of. I try to be perfect in my appearance when go to the school for a visit or a meeting. I don't want other students making fun of my kids. I looked like I can't provide for myself or them. However a lot of times I do put others before myself. I don't like to see others go without or suffer or even struggle. If I can help with a person struggle ,I will help it's just the kind of person I am, now I don't allow people to take advantage of me. But I will lend a helping hand when I can. I asked my son in law how he felt when he knew a lot of same sex relationships were in the school. He said he had to blind himself to it & pretend it wasn't there. As for my daughter she doesn't pay any attention to it she knows its there but doesn't react to it. To my nieces and nephews that went to school they say it was disgusting to see that kind of thing, it became so uncomfortable they dropped out. Now that wasn't the only reason. My nieces and nephews were so close to graduating and well they didn't finish going to school cause of the lack of encouragement there parents had and they dropped out as well. I don't know if it was the morning wake up calls that there parents got tired of , could have been the disagreements because they didn't live there lives according to the way there parents wanted them too. Maybe it could have been the fact there own bad habits got in the way of making sure there kids got an education. A lot of our past generation habits and hand me down rules have really gotten old, cause what worked for us doesn't work in this time frame. We as parents force it on our children because we don't know anything other than what we were taught. We as parents ask ourselves should I do it my mom and dads way or should I do it the way I would do it? Sometimes kids don't have a chose but to quit especially if a baby comes along. When I found out my daughter was pregnant she automatically thought she wasn't going to school, She was wrong cause I new I didn't want her missing out on all the opportunities, I did when I made that mistake. I told my daughter baby or no baby you will go to school an you will succeed wither she had liked it or not! I told her consider it being a mother with a lot of determination and a tough love That is willing and knows its best to get my kidsthe best education and they will thank me later for me pushing them to accomplish there goals. I am very proud of my kids all of them. There doing things and beginning to realize what being responsible is. My daughter just started her first job today, she is a bit nervous, but she speaks of her responsibilities when it comes to her being a student at school a mother at home and an employee at work. She tells me of how she wants to do all she can when it comes to giving her son the best. Even though she speaks of how she hates school she doesn't have far to go. She will be in the 11th grade next semester. I tell Megan before you know it you will be on stage getting handed your diploma so don't complain appreciate the education you receive . Teachers that are willing to give you the tools to survive in the world...there are times she comes home and complains about teachers, I tell her those teachers could complain about you as well, but they don't cause there to help you not complain. If the teachers had to learn how to teach the subject the students need to appreciate what all those teachers had to go through just to learn what they were taught. I'm sure they thought the very same thing .My daughter asked several of my family members what was there reasons behind there accomplishments ,or for there reason for not succeeding. My sister was forced to quit because she was expecting and the second time she tried to go back to school she believed a guy that told her he would do everything for her so she didn't need her education. She felt behind all of our failures it had to do with a man, she felt we were raising ourselves, there were some kind of abuse in there which caused us not to stay focused. She felt every time we failed it was a man in the shadows making us feel like they were controlling ,us which I can understand because it sure distracted me. I asked my friend John about his education and how did he feel about his accomplishments. He said his parents were real encouraging, he was real hard headed like teenagers seem to be at that age. AS far same sex relationships he said it wasn't in his school that it was always boy and girl. He said he had graduated in 2007 He said "he didn't know of a lot of gay students but the ones he did know he never had a problem with". I have a lot of same sex friends I don't look at them any less , the only thing that's wrong is they choose not to be involved with a partner of the opposite sex , Everyone gets upset cause they don't want to be the way we are . people don't like to accept the change In the world, They want things to be normal. well this world isn't normal ,I don't understand how can people make such a huge fuss about same sex relationships. when one has affairs they look the other way an want to pretend it's not even there. There like it's not my marriage that has that problem ,yet they continue on with life. However they make big issues about other things that has nothing to do with them, it's crazy how the world picks certain issues to make huge issues out of when there not even a part of it. I spent some time talking with my neighbor this morning and well she don't know what is wrong with our teenagers. She believes many of them want to grow up so fast and in such a huge hurry to live as an adult and there no longer listening to adults any longer. She said in her home she is pretty open about ever issue in her home and all of her children have finished school and till this day they still have open conversations and her older daughters now understand why there mother was the way she was. All have graduated and Still try being successful. She was also a child that was going through sexual abuse at home. I'm not sure most of us parents have had hardships that have cause us to fail along the way. I do feel those who were born back in the days where there were so much abuse and strict rules ,going on or parents that forced us to quit school should be able to go back to school regardless of our ages. I was 39 when I went to my local school just to go back an to be told I am too old to get an education made me feel like we only have one chance and once that chance is gone. there is no getting back! I had a 18 year old boy in my home and he goes to school with my daughter .He ask me if he could stay at my home. And as I sat down listening to his story about how his mother doesn't understand that he is gay. He has built a wall between there relationship.

He speaks of how his mother puts him down and tells him how he will never amount to anything because he is gay. I tell him its not that your mother doesn't understand its like every parents its hard for us to hear those words coming from one of our own,cause if there is ever a family reunion a parent doesn't want to have to be in a position where there having to explain why there own son or daughter chose to be gay ? They just don't want the questions no more than they want the blame. Cause they will feel they will get blamed for the road your taking or the choices and preference in who you choose to date. Some feel its an embarrassment. For others there is competition in the family where brothers ,sisters are trying to see who succeed more .who has the most money or who has the most kids to finish school or go to collage and get a degree .If you take a look one day when you get a visit from that sister or brother you haven't seen in 3 years just watch how they brag and what they wear ,when they get to your house. They will tell you everything about what they have and where they went and where they work and so on. Why cause there in competition with someone in the family or the whole family. Now not all the time, some are just happy with there success and they want to share it with loved ones. so its not all the time. In my family its a real big thing well at least some of my brothers and sisters,make it seem like it is when it really isn't. Myself personally I really don't pay any attention to it, hey if they have it happy for them if not it doesn't mean I love them any less. I don't blame anyone for anything I do have or I don't have. I have what I have because well I settled and I took a different direction in running away from the world instead of stopping to realize how much I was loosing. Now that I am an adult with children of my own I now understand why my sisters were disappointed when I chose to quit school. However I cant say they never cared about my choices . They did however I felt they were not my parents to tell me what to do, Just like any teenagers think. My sisters will never know how much I love them & how much that I get a happy when were together it may not be all of us at once but when myself,Rita,Nancy and rose get together its like having that huge yard and were like little girls running and having a great time in a way we wanted when we were growing up. To see there smiles and hear the laughter within there souls that come out of them when there laughing brings a great tear to my eyes knowing at one point in time we were all angry sisters that fought at home just for one of us being in the others room. It swells my heart to know each of us can call the other just cause we need a laugh. Because things at home are depressing are family has began to start taking life to serious. Husbands have strayed away from there wives and kids and things are no longer fun or exciting cause the husband and wife have forgotten why they married each other from the beginning , It stopped being fun , there no more dates , no more dinning , its just work, work ,work. What happen to what made the relationship. What ever happen to that spark in her eye that caught your attention the first time, what happened to that man you thought to be so fine when you were dating him? Ladies a gentlemen life isn't perfect! What now we have found some flaws in our spouses they cant make us happy any longer, I think not. We have to look for that which attracted us to each other and find that spark. Once you find it ,water your relationship . Its like a plant ,a plant needs water so it can grow. Well a relationship needs love,understanding, and trust as well as conversation in it in order for it to develop . Stop worrying about all those small weeds. Cause when your love for each other starts growing eventually those weeds will die. It reminds me of a friend of mine named Zackariah. He is 19 In The medical field . He asked me what was wrong with him? I said not a thing. Why? Well he feels he will never be loved by anyone. I tell him he has a whole life ahead of him. It will come, He asked me how he would know if its the right person. I told him well u wont feel doubt. Your emptiness within your soul will be filled, You will feel you and her are inseparable. You cant eat, cant sleep kinda of thing. Sometimes it will feel as if your flying without wings. You will just know. He longs for a true love at such a young age. I wonder why Zackariah would be thinking about this ? Is it cause he feels empty inside that he will never find a mate? He tells me he feels lonely. Like there is a huge void and feels only a girl can fill that void. I don't know how true it is. But He is searching. He feels his parents are strict on him and they don't understand. I Tell him its not that your parents don't understand. They have been places you haven't an when you have a career ,the last thing your parents want is for you to get involved in situations that will hurt your career later. There just looking out for your health and well being. Zackariah feel he knows what he is doing and adults much older cant tell him anything because he knows. If all these angry teens really new half of what us grown ups knew They would want to really slow down.

So many have rushed through there lives by running away from home to live with someone they believed they loved at one point. I Don't believe that most us ran away from home to be with the one we felt we were in love with, I do believe most us ran away to be with our partners out of desperation or escape from the abuse or neglect we suffered at home. So there we have settled for less than our self worth. Cause most us didn't believe we could ever have anyone good in our lives so we couldn't wait We just got involved feeling the safety and the comfort we never received at home. Therefore we got involved and made that safety and comfort our relationship. Which leads to a rapid failed relationship. I tell my daughter Cassandra who has been in a relationship with a guy she has only known for year. Cassandra had a son with this guy within a years time. However she didn't give herself time to get to know this guy for who really was. When she started living with him it seem to her they were in love. It was he was willing to provide for her , which she over looked the souls and heart. She didn't get to know the man behind the scene sort of speak. But now that she is really living with him he now shows her the abuser in himself as well as the selfish negative person he is. He has kept her in a state of depression for a year and manage to keep her away from her family and people who really loves her. He never wanted her to associate with anyone who was encouraging or gave her advice ,that could be positive in her life. He was taking away the very thing that would help her to succeed in life. Her family was forced to be at a distant because of his evil ways and rude control. She would be home everyday with only a cell phone as her contact outside her home . She was not allowed to leave . If she wanted to talk to anyone it had to be when he left home . The moment he would arrive home Cassandra had to hang the phone up or his evil side would erupt. Seemed like he would just find a reason to become angry just to leave my daughter just so he could sleep in another woman's bed. I would listen to my daughter as she would tell me his routine when it would come to him coming home early hours in the morning just to wash off his hours of sexual lust. I told my daughter he was having a affair. As much as it hurt me to tell her. But when you have been around it as much as I have I know the signs very well. I hear how my daughter sheds tears cause she wants so much to find her a real true love. She doesn't understand how men can hurt a woman in that manner. Well like I tell her women can hurt a man the same way. There are so many reasons that men and women have used to have affairs. But not one man or woman can ever say , I didn't get to really know you like I should have and I missed getting to know your heart and soul or personally. I don't want to hurt you so I have to let you go cause I have the desire to meet someone else. No one will ever be that honest with themselves or with there partners, When it comes to a relationship well some of us really need to take a good look and ask why there's no more candles lit in our relationship or where have all the roses gone. At times our lives have become such a normal thing we forget about that person at home that we claim to be that special someone. Like right now, its Sunday the 11th of April we went to pick my daughter up from Temple, Texas her boyfriend was being disruptive .So my daughter called me to go pick her up. We drove down there picked her up and brought her back to Waco, Texas with us. Well we were getting ready for bed. I came to my bedroom it had been months since my husband had a sexual romance with me at all. I had suspected something however I had no proof of that so I kept letting the issue in my mind about it go. However it was 2a.m I was fixing to go to bed and something kept telling me to get his cell phone. I always thought it was weird he stopped putting it on the charger in the house , he would take it to work charge it there. And he would always lock it in the glove compartment and after I asked my husband why he kept it in the glove compartment he said well its so I wont forget it when I go to work. Which I thought was a bunch of bull crap anyway. When he started leaving it in the glove compartment I had sense that he was talking and seeing someone else. Again I just didn't have the proof. But this night I was going to bed I got his car keys went to his car opened up the glove compartment , I turned his cell phone on , I began to browse through his pictures and there were nude pictures of the other woman . I also went through all his text messages and seeing messages of I love you from the other woman and it had tore me up ,I was angry & questioning why?? What did I do to deserve this? I was in the living room when this happened after seeing this I ran to the bedroom where he laid asleep and I said loudly well, well what do we have here. He jumped up as drunk as he was and sobered up in a huge hurry All he could say was Liza! What are u doing with my cell phone! He didn't even have time to think about his answers or anything , not that I gave him the chance anyway. I seen this cold look on his face like he was relived it was out! Now he looks like he can have everything he wants without a care in the world. Still no response. Ladies and men I'm going to tell you . To protect your relationship and family. If you and your husband ,boyfriends have a cell phone . Pick a day out of the blue to exchange cell phones go through it and see if there is anything he or she has been hiding from you. If your partner has nothing to hide they will give it up without a problem if they don't there hiding an affair. Cell phones are another huge problem in a relationships , we don't mind having one because of the trust, but that cell phone is another way to have a affair. So everyone take notes. Just say to your partner out of the blue hand it over and start scrolling and see what you find. Another thing to watch out for is if there going to the restroom more than usual half of the time there texting in the restroom or taking pictures of themselves. See if there phone is always kept on vibration or silent , that's to keep you from knowing there receiving calls from someone else. If they begin hiding there cells you already know something is going on. I sit here everyday since I found out my husband was having a affair an watch as he mopes and feels so depressed after I found out about this. Now he wants out he signed the divorce papers cause now he thinks the grass is greener and he is fixing to get a wake up call. His unfaithfulness is the reason for his relationships getting ruined he doesn't want help , he feels he needs no one to tell him what is wrong with him , cause he feels he is always right. His past break ups have been his reason for hurting every woman he has ever been with he thinks he is destined to be alone. Some men usually are especially when they have a tendency to have affairs just like a woman. However its up to both parties to seek help and deal with those issues so they wont continue on in life hurting people who don't deserve to be hurt. They take it out on the ones who have stood by and love them to the depths of there souls just to crush there spirits after years of loving and caring. Talk about a raw deal. I asked my daughter who is 17 years old what she thought about affairs she doesn't believe its right and people that are married should stay away from temptation and just be faithful. If only it was that easy. I do believe a man or woman should be court ordered to wear wedding rings if they are married in a church or court of law. Regardless where they work. There are some jobs where men are not allowed to wear a ring. Which I feel is breaking a marriage law. I do believe they should make a law where if your married and your not wearing a ring , you should be fined for it. To avoid infidelity ,So many relationships are broken cause a men or woman go around saying there single when in fact they are married. So therefore they sleep around destroying others relationships and homes all because they cant say I'm sorry but I'm Married. I have one of my daughters with me and her name is Cassandra I asked her what she thousght about same sex relationships? She said in her High school the guys would do it undercover. People don't have open conversation about it in the town where she lived. As far as her relationships she feels Love is a Battle Field ,cause some guys carry there past hurts with them and interferes with there relationships it can either get worse or better but if neither the man or woman seeks help , there area there relationships will always go sour. If you or a Family is in need of concealing or help dealing with issues such as Abuse call your nearest abuse hotline . Get help. I walk around right now trying to figure out where I went wrong with my husband . I don't know if it was my past hurts that I carried into this relationship. However after talking to my husband I figured out it was his past hurts , he tells me story of his first love and how she left and never come back to him, He was planning to Marry her. Then his second relationship he found out his girlfriend was sleeping with his family members . Then he says how he remember how his mom would take his dad back all the time just to turn around and hurt him again. How he remembers his dad always begging and pleading with her. His Dad past away about 4 yrs ago and my husband said he died loving one woman and no one ever replaced her in his heart. I sit down with my husband I hear as he talks about other woman and his reaction in his eyes. With a hunger for more than just me. It hurts as I hear this, but I keep seeing my life away from him as he disrespects me. I feel he laughs as he makes me feel beneath him as if I am no one to him as if we never shared 9 years together. I feel he is heartless and he is only out to get what he wants and doesn't care who he has to step on to get it. All his brothers are the same way not faithful. Basically your male whore. No respect for women at all. He has a brother that has one girlfriend but sees two other women on the side and he takes them all 3 to visit his mom. I find it rude and disrespectful. And there mom says nothing. My husband feels its his mothers fault for being the way he is. However I was always taught to be responsible for the things we do.

Using his mom as an excuse I feel is a cop out! He is just plan heartless. It hurts me to a point knowing a man really never knows what he has until its gone! I guess for some that's true. Just not for the men and women that go around behaving as if there untouchable. I feel some are made of stone. Not even hugging the ones they hurt. Not even a little sympathy or remorse for what they have done. What will become of our hearts our souls and wounds and past pains. Will our pains ever be Truly healed..... I have Zachary visiting us today and I am going to ask him about his views on his childhood. As for as school his parents wanted Zachary to get his education. His parents didn't make it difficult, he felt he was smart and he always felt he could do better than his parents expected him too as long as he set his mind to it. Zachary always felt he was treated differently by his mom. Zachary thought about asking his mom why she treated him different however he didn't care to know. He kept going to school. When he reached middle school he seen the student in that school were highly sexual and were not ashamed to show affection towards there girlfriends or boyfriends. Zachary was in high school when he began seeing same sex relationships. When he seen this he felt Love had no boundaries. He has also heard of relationships where there is domestic abuse. I asked him how he felt about it he feels it psychological , Zachary feels it doesn't make it OK for a woman or man to get beat. He also feels that every struggle that he has makes him strive to go further. Because he works in a clinic he felt that working in a retirement home gave him the hunger to continue helping others. As far as the family relationship Zachary feels there is a void in his life. He doesn't know why & he has never got passed it. He said he would never want to know why his mom treats him different , he continues to say it is what it is. Zachary thinks relationships when it comes to someone being unfaithful, he claims he would never be unfaithful. He feels that we all have to go through certain things in order to get where were going in the next life. He feels life is what a person makes of it. He also feels when it comes to his own life , Zachary makes it difficult for himself. Because of his thinking. I told Zachary he needed to control his mind or his mind will control him. He feels he doesn't know how to Love a woman as in affectionate towards them. He feels he only will have to learn as he goes. He walks away with tears in his eyes . He doesn't know if his family members were to die today , he doesn't know if he would feel bad about it. I tell him if there are things you want to say to your mom, dad or sister and you don't say it to them when there alive , you will have to carry that guilt because you never said what u should have now that there gone. Seldom people cross our paths for a reason. And if you don't take advantage of the chance when its in front of you , you will never have that chance again , cause tomorrow is never promised to anyone. He seems somewhat relived as he wipes tears away from his eyes. He speaks to my daughters and tells her how he feels the family love being in our home. Makes me feel good to know someone can feel that in our home. I really don't like people being in my home. I don't have friends ,especially female friends , cause they either try to come on and make passes at our husband or your husband tries to come on to them. I cant trust anyone. Because of the men I have been with they have either mistreated the trust we had with there infidelities or domestic issues drinking or drugs. Yes, I want to fall in Love again Will I marry again, Yes , however my next choosing will be careful. I hate the marriage I have now , I have to pretend around my husbands friends that all is well. He gives me fake kisses and hugs in front of his family. When we get home its back to the same old thing arguments and repeats of our divorce. I was telling my daughter how I cant stand that I have to live in the same house with a man I am married too, knowing he cant stand me or doesn't even want to be around me. I will never understand how a human being can be so heartless like we never were married. I find myself sometimes begging and pleading with tears that no longer swell in my eyes. I ask myself what happened to all my tears? Its like I no longer have any to shed over someone who just wants what he wants and that's it! He fell in love with another married woman for the fourth time & again he cant have her. Why? Cause I am in his way. Therefore he feels sleeping on the edge of the bed will make him feel single again. He does this as a respect towards his female lover. He has no respect for me or my thoughts. I see at times the way he hugs my daughter and I hear the way he tells his daughters he loves them. I cant help but roll my eyes and say ,How can u love anyone when you cant love your wife. I cant see my husband with anyone else, But the more I think about leaving him I think about how I no longer have to put up with his crap! Like his immature ways ,drinking and the ways he disrespects me in front of his family and friends speaking of other women he sees. I tell my husband one day you will find someone who will be unfaithful break your heart and soul and you will never recover from those wounds , because of all the hurt you have inflicted on your wife. He walks around cold not willing to talk . He only waits for 1:30 to come around so he can rush off to work. Sad to say but its true, I have never heard of a man rushing off to get away from his wife. I thought a man enjoyed being in a woman's arms. In his case that's every woman's arms. I find it sick,degrading, and rude ! If a man cant be faithful I highly recommend he never marries, People get hurt as well as children & its not fair!Men just like women have a tendency of having affairs without the thought of who all is involved .They don't go to a motel with the person there having an affair with and discuss the people they are going to hurt. Do you think any man or woman that has an affair actually think about there husband or wife at home? Do you think they even consider there at home with worry wondering where there at? No, they don't care! They would rather sit in a room with someone they hardly know not knowing if they have STDs,making up excuses to this person why they are unhappy or what there husbands or wives don't do for them or complain about what they don't get sex wise In the bedroom . There are so many women that go out with a man just cause there not wearing a ring. Hello ladies News Flash! Not all married men wear a ring cause they still consider themselves single when there not. There looking for easy women & Nothing more & ladies unfaithful men will never leave there wives for you. These men are on the prowl collecting stars to see how many women they can have sex with and how many women they can brag about. And ladies if your sending nude pictures of yourself to a guys cell phone. 9 times out of 10 there showing that picture to half of the city you are from. If you feel your spouse will never find out about your affair well I'm living proof we married husbands and wives will always find out one way or another. My husband had 4 affairs and I found out about all of them!Did he ever divorce me for any of them "No". He may have told them that, but where is he? Still in my bed. Before you think about sleeping around you better do some investigating ask the man for there house number see if they give it to you. If they don't they live with a woman which means there married. Ask to go to there house. If they give you some excuse, there married. If the only place you can talk is a work parking lot,a park or motel there married. Ladies yawl need to start playing it safe and smart. There are men now days that don't care as long as we ladies choose to spread our legs for free or just a little sweet talk they will get there's any way they can .Men the same applies if you want to know if a woman is married ask for her house number not just her cell. Ask to go to her house. To both men & women if nothing else call the records dept and ask if that person is married. In all my relationships I have been educated real well about the hide and seek game of affairs. I know what women and men do and how they do it. Its getting so bad a married person cant even go shopping at a grocery store without trying to meet someone. Now don't misconstrue what I am saying. I am not saying all men or women do this. I am only speaking of those that are unfaithful. My husband meets women at work,parking lots, while getting gas. Especially when he goes places alone. He gives women this certain look and then smiles says hello and begins conversation gets a number if he can. He even has side jobs he does he meets women through his side jobs. Nothing is completely business all the time. Men if your at work and you have a woman at home everyday or women if you have a man that stays home everyday , check into it. He/she may have some extra company. You know the expression when the cats away the mouse will play. Well the mouse sometimes has a full house. Some women and men when they find out about affairs there in shock! And like me I begin to wonder what I could of done that would have changed this from ever happening , my husband tells me its not me ,its himself .He would like to be faithful but cant!So he feels letting me go is safer. Cause he doesn't want to hurt me any longer. He is aware he may have another affair. However he chooses not to seek help. He would prefer to run away from his issues than deal with the issues in front of him. We all have daily work and bills that have to be done. We get so focused on all this ,we fail to realize who we neglect and then were shocked when they look for someone else to ease there loneliness. I am not saying its right. But there are two people at fault. Ourselves for the neglect and the spouse for not trusting us enough to talk to us about how they felt. I don't care how lonely your partner is ,They should trust there mates enough to go to them even if there lonely. I know sometimes I hear ,But we always argue. Well arguing will never resolve anything cause no one is listening. Sometimes just sit on the bed and let your partner know in a civil manner we really need to talk. If they care enough they will. Don't beg ,just ask. If they tell you they don't have time. Then they cant be shocked when you go to someone other than themselves. Partners go to someone else cause there own responds in a argumentative way. Which frightens the other not to even say a word at all. Leaving them feeling lonely , neglected and unable to speak to there partners. Its especially hard when you are a in-law and your family lives out of town. And you have no family to talk to without them telling you 'I Told you so".We need comfort not the who is to blame. Its the both of yawl. Sometimes we need to really scan our relationships. No one can really blame the other. Its all about Conversation. If its not there, it will never work. Break the cycle of past grudges or our past will always follow...

About the Author

Eloisa Aguillon Perez was born in Cameron. Texas, on March 20, 1970 to a Mr. Alfred Aguillon & Mary Aguillon. I am a mother of 4 children & 2 Grandchildren. I left home at the age of 16 seeking Escape from the world of Sexual Abuse and Domestic Violence. My past experinces have made me the Strong Woman I am today. My Sisters Nancy, Patricia, Rita, Josie, Rose, Mary &  Dinna have been my inspiration when it came to me writting this book. Our story was never told. I felt we were owed some closure that we never received growing up. And this is my way of Gaining some Closure and Comfort for me & my Sisters. I would like to Especially Thank My Editors Megan Balboa And Roman Ramos for making this possible for me as Well As AuthorHouse. I would like to Also say a Special Thank You to a Kenneth Teague for being my best friend & helping me to belive I can do anything i set my mind to.